HOME VISIT

Home Visit
© Michal Rubin / Cathexis Northwest Press

No part of this book may be reproduced without written permission of the
publisher or author, except in reviews and articles.

First Printing: 2023

ISBN: 978-1-952869-86-0

Editing & Design by C. M. Tollefson
Cathexis Northwest Press

cathexisnorthwestpress.com

HOME VISIT

Poetry by Michal Rubin

Cathexis Northwest Press

10/15/2023

From the South Carolina patio I watch news from my other home, Israel, counting the dead after seven days of war that is flooding homes, streets...all ground my feet knew so well, and the ground of our neighbors, where my feet have not traveled.

The poems in this collection have been written throughout the past couple of years, and are in no way an up-to-the-minute record of the events unfolding between Israel and Palestine. They are but my reflection and the expression of my own battle between my attachment to Israel, the home of my childhood, and my heart ache over Israeli politics as it relates to the Palestinian people. I have long been torn between leaving Israel and loving it, all while facing the truth and deceptions in the telling of its modern history. The poems weave a story of finding refuge and home of one peoples while losing refuge and homes for another peoples.

Today, as I write this forward, the map of my wrestling is plastered on every news outlet, across social media, and on the faces of my friends and family. I recollect my childhood fears of my imagined atrocities of war as I sat in a bomb shelter, a twelve-year-old with my mother and our neighbors. Then later in the day, I face my very adult fears of antisemitism intermingled with my shame and pain for my country's behavior in the occupied Palestinian territories. The fears are no longer painted in muted, careful colors, but in a garish bold cruelty. The visions of atrocities that were fears of a twelve-year-old, no longer are imagined fears but the reality of the savagery my people and our neighbors are drowning in. My poems are a telling of my small corner of this story of two peoples who have lost their way and continue to wander in the desert of the human shadows. May we find a way to see the humanity of each other.

Table of contents

I am the field of their wars	1
Carolina/Al-Tuwani	3
The glass blower	5
There Here	6
Omar Abdalmajeed As'ad of Jiljilya	7
In Gaza	10
Demolition	11
I speak not your language she said to the boy	15
Ben Gurion Boulevard	16
I see the seed-man's cart	17
Useful	18
Crumbled	20
Home Visit	24
In an Empty Lot Between Two Buildings	27
Fourteen trees on Ben Gurion Blvd or Interment	28
Epilogue	29

I am the field of their wars

sandal-wrapped feet
steps draw
the path
upon me
thus I am known

                and taken
                and fought over
                grabbed in a fist
                clutched by hands

they want me
I bear the weight
their yearning
I soak up their blood
and stay arid

                I am the witness
                the lover
                the stolen
                the given
                the taken

                the promised

                the object
                the prize
                lost and
                found

sandal-wrapped
feet draw
upon me

                take me
                share me
                steal me
                dream of me
                leave me

I speak
with my breath
they don't hear

                        I am the witness
                            the prize
                            the lover
                            the stolen
                            the given
                            the taken

I am the mother of
Abel and Cain
Yishma – El and Yitzchak
the storyteller
of their lives
I am the field
of their wars

                        I am the womb
                        of their graves

Carolina/Al-Tuwani

I

On Yom Kippur
we say
For the sins we have committed against you by resorting to violence
For the sins we have committed against you by greed and oppressive interest
For the sins we have committed against you by plotting against others

II

Friday.
A pot filled with soil
from a Miracle-Gro plastic bag
holds the Creeping Jenny
which adorns it,
a dress with its matching scarf
trailing
green
leaf after green leaf
a Carolina patio
six thousand miles from Al-Tuwani
A day after Yom Kippur

the water hose bursting with
pressure
spraying its abundance
as each leaf bows
engorged
green
joining its sisters in a
parade of beauty
six thousand miles from Al-Tuwani
A day after Yom Kippur

III

Friday.
An email bridges six thousand miles
in one click,
a water transport to
South Hebron Hills-
Al Tuwani-
The village
awaits water
from a tank clouded by dust
The southwest wind
sees not
the absence of abundance

six thousand miles from Carolina
A day after Yom Kippur

The imprisoned water,
locked in the shining tank
adorned with green and black
banner
"Access to Water for All"
a vision
a plea
an impossible demand
in South Hebron Hills

Water is permitted on
Tuesday, Wednesday and Thursday

Today is Friday
A day after Yom Kippur

IV

I sink into the green of
the Carolina patio
hiding in the humidity
of shame
six thousand miles from Al-Tuwani
the Friday after Yom Kippur
For the sins we are committing against You
I mumble

The glass blower

I watch his silhouette
against the furnace.
Tawfiq, he said his name, f
rom Hebron.
An art fair
seventy-two hundred miles
from the last checkpoint.
His accent carries the taste,
the nakedness
his last strip search.

He forms the vase,
turns the punty.
His defiance blown
into molten glass
in the fire.
Blue and green
of the Mediterranean
become a dwelling
to his history
a sphere around his blown words:

my daughter
in 22 years
has not seen the sea

the roadblocks
no permit
nothing changes

"blown" like the chanted words
of well-meaning protesters
carried by the winds
to the nowhere of the desert

There

The soccer ball rolled
behind the pile
awaiting the muffled
footsteps chasing it
grabbing its dusted skin
leftover from the rubble
onto which it rolled

Here

The blanket is dragged
on the concrete,
underground
it has a smell, she notices,
learning to fall asleep
with bombs
in the background

Omar Abdalmajeed As'ad of Jiljilya

Haaretz newspaper reports
3am
Omar Abdalmajeed As'ad is stopped by Israeli soldiers on his drive home, after spending time with friends.

the moon is smiling, oblivious to the rattled
heart   thumping against the white shirt
buttoned tightly over a late-night dinner
of rice and maybe thick lamb stew

3:05am
The soldiers demand that As'ad step out of his vehicle. They argue with him for 15 minutes.

Hebrew and Arabic mingle in a snake-like dance
or a sword fight with only one sword
and one victor

always
the same one wins

3:20 am
The soldiers walk As'ad to an abandoned yard, where they handcuff him, lay him on the ground, gag him and blindfold him.

the rancid aroma of cumin and cinnamon, the
leftover flavor of friends, permeates the thick
gag with a terrifying intimacy of living in a dream
of dying on the cold dusty ground

3:35am
Soldiers lead two more detainees to the yard. One of them notices As'ad is lying still on his stomach.

his full stomach is pressed against the small pebbles
as 78-year-old skin surrenders to the indentations
branding As'ad
declaring the kinship of man and land
as the almost full moon still is in oblivion

3:45am
Two more detainees are brought to the yard. No one is handcuffed apart from As'ad.

his hands bound to each other clutch fleetingly
moments stored in his wilting veins
toddlers joyfully
squealing   love   making
lamb stew   sweetness of pistachio-
filled baklawa

4am
The soldiers free one of As'ad's hands and leave the yard.

not bound together the hands no longer harbor
As'ad's stored moments
they "rest" upon the spillage of his life
leaving handprints
branding the earth
the kinship of land and man

4:09am
One of the detainees calls a doctor after noticing As'ad is unresponsive and his face has turned blue.

no flickering of the moonlight to mark
the moment As'ad's blindfolded eyes   dimmed
the absence of air bluing
the wrinkled face

stillness

4:10am
A doctor arrives at the yard from a nearby clinic and tries to resuscitate As'ad.

the white shirt ripped   dusted
with the land   no longer white
and new hands part the sea
of stillness in a futile effort
to infuse life into
this body   an empty vessel

zip tie on its wrist

4:20am
As'ad is brought to the clinic and medics continue to treat him.

neon flares   no more   moonlight
frenetic world life-sustaining measures   violent
clanking desperation against As'ad's bare chest

desecrate the holy stillness
of dying at dawn

4:40am
The doctor pronounces As'ad's death

One commander will be
rebuked

two subordinate company and platoon commanders will be
dismissed

As'ad is buried in his village Jiljilya

In Gaza

tomorrow's touch
through the settling dust

will remind you of
love

unhidden in the rubble
behind the corner

forbidden moment
fused with desert breeze

salted droplets we carried
home

        or what was home

Demolition

***

she stood holding a pillow
clutching the tail of her
shirt

peering through
the toppled window frame
open

onto the gray concrete heap
the edge of the torn red curtain
unveils

echoes of bulldozers wrecking
her father's hunched body
held

by the groove of dismayed land
a son's hand
resting

on dusty hair yearning
to fix his father's
brokenness

at a distance a soldier's bored
stare thunders upon the arid
hills

she stood holding a pillow
clutching onto the engraved
memory

***

***

Truth comes in early morning

no bed to lie in

to be demolished

gray print, gray paper

bulldozer creeps into its ravaging self

a suitcase lost in the rubble

girl holding a pillow

what died is in a heap

the soldier cursed with

echoes   wrecking

no door to exit

in his shroud

standing   bored

in oblivion

no power to object

beneath   death creeps in

***

***

Fifty-two weeks—Number of demolished structures: 957; number of girls who lost their homes: 235;

        Grooved arid soil lay
        beneath the rubble holding
        silent displaced screams

number of women who were displaced: 258; number of boys who became homeless: 276;

echoes of wrecking
shroud a wilted soldier's soul
boredom masks brokenness

number of men whose houses were bulldozed: 288;

gray rubble gray dust
gray hair gray tears gray sunray
rest on torn red drape

number of affected people due to demolished structures: 28,474; number of red torn curtains: ~ 2,015

I write my red screams
over crumbled soul of boy-
soldier lost and gray

number of clothes-filled bundles; ~ maybe 3,000; number of keys without doors: estimated 3,525

I dream of him bent
torn red curtain receives his
awoken brokenness

number of concrete heaps: 957.

***

***

somewhere in South Hebron Hills there is a girl holding a pillow

a pillow, torn red curtain, concrete heap   remnants
        fifty-two weeks nine hundred fifty-seven concrete heaps
                echoes of my rage dance within the walls of Carolina's comfort

a broken father fills his pockets with his shame
        gray rubble gray dust gray sunrays color the forgotten
                I write my red screams in the deafness of here

the bulldozer has no pockets and no shame   wrecking
        in the gray dust a soldier is cursed   being there is etched
                the radio mumbles lies and I wonder how could they

a toddler son   hunched over torn gray curtain
        three thousand keys scattered on concrete piles without doors
                dinner hummus   labneh   Carolina kitchen
                shards of sentimental food   pennants to the distance

somewhere in South Hebron Hills there is a girl holding a pillow

***

I speak not your language she said to the boy

I, born from the womb of
my mother's remembrances
wrapped in the cocoon
of her story

                                        you, amongst the trees, the earth
                                        below littered with unpicked olives
                                        the story of Hagar and Yishmael
                                        is your womb

my skin a scroll,
an epic of what was
like tombstones
etched with numbers

                                        the remains of the broken down
                                        home in the arid field pasture
                                        your diary
                                        carved in the stone

                                        You laugh in pleasure
                                        your small act of defiance
                                        your urine naturally marks your
                                        territory which
                                        I have marred

I feel its warmth running down
my sweaty shirt
my tongue tied in shame

                                        you are telling your story

I speak not your language
and it's 2pm
the radio announcer
reads out names of
lost relatives,
maybe they have survived

                                        yours, they live in a tent
                                        somewhere
                                        without radio announcements
                                        you guard the stones
                                        that have survived

Ben Gurion Boulevard

My feet hugged and pulled away from the concrete sidewalk tiles
pretending to be cool, walking barefoot to the beach, the same
beach where I want my ashes scattered.   The blisters
a cushion, an added bounce to my steps.   I loved them.
The sidewalks. The grout joints, dirty, making sure to skip over.
The blisters. The pain. Spartan perseverance. Walking on hot coals.
Words are steps on hot coals.
            And I throw more words into the mix.

My concrete. My sidewalk. My smoldering path. I knew it like I knew the bottom
of my feet and the street corner where the blisters would be unveiled.
Like words, or some truths I can't hide. Eruptions.
No more cushions, now sharp objects, litter strewn on the edge of a tile,
the stink of smeared dog feces, unpicked, like stinging words no one wants
to hear, strewn on the page, waiting to be stepped on.
            And I throw more words into the mix. Stepping on hot coals.

My street. Its gray hue   a blend of cracks and holes, misconceptions, or simply
lies about its smoothness. Unlike the glazed stories I read in third grade printed
on sleek paper with a flower at the corner. Still on my bookshelf sixty years later.
Like the smell of the bus fumes permeating my barefoot walk.   Still resting
in the recesses   of my memory.   Words are steps on hot coals.

I see the seed-man's cart

He parks his cart at the corner of Reines St. and Ben Gurion Boulevard, his unshaved face unchanged from the week before. You never ask for his name. All you know is that he comes from an Arab village and you wonder if his son will be here today to help weigh the 150gr of salted unhulled sunflower seeds and 50gr of salted roasted unhulled pumpkin seeds that are way harder to peel and spit the husks, definitely not with the same efficiency as the sunflower seeds.

There is an art to eating unhulled sunflower seeds. The speed and accuracy of biting, the coordination of the teeth and tongue to crack the shell, fish the seed, chew it, and spit the shell accurately into the bowl. The dissolving salt, later mixed with the sip of grapefruit juice is the taste of Friday afternoon, as city buses begin their rest, the fumes land on the sidewalk, there is an emptying of sounds only to allow the 4pm news from the neighbor's radio to colonize the entering Sabbath.

Not good news. Usually. You continue to spit the hulls of the seeds, sip the grapefruit juice straight from the large bottle, and tune in to the names of the dead from the last terror attack. The pile of spent hulls in the bowl is growing. You look at it with a level of pride, for a moment think of the sunflower-seed-vendor from the Arab village who is so mild mannered and gentle. The 5pm news from the neighbor's radio penetrates the sip of grapefruit juice.

Useful

it is my feet that are marked with the imprint of the land
they carried me with an obedience of a uniformed body
though I was not one to be modeled after
as a fine specimen of a soldier.

but my feet were.

they took me to places my reckless mind commanded,
bare or shoed.
the feet obedient to my living in the love affair.
Land   feet   recklessness   obedience

truth   I thought

of winter my feet
squished onto
the soaked shoes
filled with first rain

water

the cherished commodity
pooled
in murky puddles
of uneven sidewalks

the galoshes stayed dry at home waiting for an opportunity
to be useful

I mean
a small new country needed us to be useful
always
and we were

usefully knowing names of trees and birds
geographical details we collected
in Homeland classes
skillful recitation of poetry in memorial ceremonies

mostly
feeling at home

cozy with all that's familiar
and is just ours

I thought

all that my feet introduced me to
as they carried me   through
remains of cultures
stones told stories

of two thousand years
one thousand years
five hundred years
twenty-year- old stories

the young and exotic stones
became homes
to new inhabitants
there were no ghosts

I thought

my feet loved the sea, the one they wanted to drive us into
       so we disappear
the sharp edges of seashells   a reminder
but I laughed. And that was useful.   To believe we will not disappear.

We are still sunning on the shores
of that sea, decades later,
laughter mired in the perpetual war
but our presence is useful

Crumbled

1948,   Genya and Henryk—fractured testimony—

promised   an apartment,   they gave us
a key   at Jaffa   near the harbor   a house   we
opened the gate,   couldn't believe our eyes...   shock.
The house   beautiful but   in the yard   a round
table   set   dusty plates,   not for us   ...we were frightened.

it hurt us,   it   reminded us   we had to leave
everything   when the Germans arrived   threw us into the ghetto.
the same situation,   and it was not in us to stay. ... ...
did not want to do the same thing that the Germans did.

my childhood storybook of imagined truth   no longer in the museum
     yellowed in the naked sun   crumbled
gone to dust

no one
         dared
      to publicly speak
            of how Israel
      had expelled
                Palestinians

1954
Israeli parliament   Constitution, Law and Justice Committee

Chanan Rubin   member

Members ▮ ▬▬▬▬▬ *wake up!*

my father's words

▮ המצב כמו שנהווה   אין לשאתו עוד
▬▬▬▬▬▬ אין לנו זכות מוסרית לשלול
טענות צודקות של
▬▬▬▬ הערביים במדינת ישראל.
לא ייתכן שבמדינת ישראל ייקחו אדמות
▬▬▬▬ של אנשים ▮ בארץ ▮
▮   ▬▬▬▬ על מנת לעשות
עסקים מפוקפקים

Unbearable   it is
▮ *inconceivable* ▮
the State of Israel,
▬▬▬▬   *takes land homes* ▮
▬▬▬▬ ▬▬ ▬▬
from those ▬▬▬▬
who own ▮ *the land.*
Take it away,
profit from
▬▬▬▬▬▬

what's not
yours

1960

        no one
                                      dares
    to publicly speak
                we
                                    had expelled
            Palestinians

        I was so young

2022

Israel's high court has ruled
            1,000 Palestinians can be evicted   land repurposed   military use,
                              single biggest expulsion

                    Al Markaz village West Bank   The Najjar family knew

                          May 11

a neighbor called: "*The bulldozer is coming.*"

                        The court   unswayed

the Najjars' house   demolished,

"*We had 30 minutes to get out what we could,*" she said
                                                        She   looked over
pile of broken blocks   twisted metal   her family home

"It took no time and our house was gone."

The Geneva conventions *it is illegal*
    to expropriate occupied land
        to forcibly transfer the local population.

The high court   green-lighted   population transfer

Deportation of over 1,000 people

                       a   humanitarian

catastrophe

I am
        not young

                 anymore

Home Visit

First evening

                        immersed in the warmth
                        of childhood aromas of caramelized
                        onions from the neighbors' kitchen
                        my mind caressing my mother's
                        new wrinkles in the midst
                        of an assault
                        television news
Not new

Where was the attack today?
How many?   Pictures.
The funerals of yesterday's
dead.   Wailing mothers.   Fathers Collapsing.

Don't miss a word, a detail.
The television brings the bodies home.

Monosyllable
anguish.

Relieved I was not
on that bus today.

The next morning

The names of yesterday's victims
transform the newspaper
a "yearbook" with last words
uttered before death
under photos   stills

An updated count of the dead.

Second evening

Television assaults
with Names.
Noa Orbach, 18-year-old
Shiran Nechmad, 7-year-old
Aharon Ben Israel, 32-year-old

Five Palestinians

nameless

Where was the attack today?
How many? Blood   glass   concrete shards
The funerals of yesterday's
dead.   Wailing mothers.

Brothers and sisters holding each other.

Television brings the bodies home.

Monosyllable
anguish.

Relieved I was not
at the mall today

Third evening

        Immersed in the warmth
        of childhood aromas of caramelized onions
        from the neighbors' kitchen
        watching my mother's wrinkles
        move with the agony
        of television news

Not new

A talk-show discussion
of the loss of empathy
for the Other Side
Innocent Palestinian victims have

      no names
           no faces

The guests mourn what
we have lost. The slow death of our
morality.

I feel pride.
We dare to face our
failings.

We are running out of time the host says

thirty minutes

(dedicated to
our moral failings)

And then
a commercial break

In an Empty Lot Between Two Buildings

It started below.   The ground met the feet and crawled up with the memory of heat, water, the smell of fried falafel   as if the soil infusing life into my legs and I become or return to before   the moment of being formed,
clay emerging   with a story   from the empty lot between two buildings.
There I carry with me the grains of earthen smell,   taste of boiled and peppered chickpeas.
          I stop there,   a statue.   Like Lot's wife halting.   Tuning into sounds of life from the forbidden   distant untouchable   holding the life
of the memories   and the images carved onto the clay my skin a canvas to the epic.

What did she want   Lot's wife   leaving and   not leaving   staying afar unseparated separated   the music from Sodom continued to flow in her   solid body shivered   hair bristles with each note   she wanted to touch and stay afar
         reaching forward   and backward   dwelling in the purgatory of yearning   missing escaping recalling and calling.   She is there in the empty lot between the two buildings.   I silently call her   we meld   joined millennia ago   we gaze into somewhere   the words mingle inside   unending and unformed flow of lava pent up me and Lot's wife   in an empty lot between two buildings

Fourteen trees on Ben Gurion Blvd
or
Interment

carry my ashes along the boulevard counting
the trees along the way as I did in the pre-ash
state
love me there at the shores of childhood
with the urn's contents eager to join the
sea
speckles on the surface of the water
the green and blue
a calm
that coats what's beneath

the ripples sway the specks of me
a cradle hushing the surface
 words
and I   slowly   speck a fter s peck
sink down into where I was born
and was meant to
stay

engulfed by what I had
left

returning
to the salt-water

rinsing
the crystals off my folds

the speckles off the surface
of my life

rinsing
the reminders

of the distance

from home

Epilogue

10/15/2023 | Rabi'I 30, 1445 AH | 30 th of Tishrei, 5784

will there be a day
tomorrow

there is a silence ~~of horror~~
not knowing where to go
whom to talk to
what to say
which words are forbidden
which feelings need to melt
melt with the pain
melt into the day it is
into a tomorrow

and the blue sky of fall

will there be more ~~videos~~
slayed babies in their cribs
posts of the raped
last words broken
will there be a day

after tomorrow

and the blue sky of fall

swastikas or celebrations ~~of atrocities~~
celebrations
heinous acts
as if they are liberating

will tomorrow be
trail of tears
of the homeless
between the bleeding ground
and the blue sky of fall

the fall of the fallen ~~hopes~~
the fall of all falls

Thanks to the editors of the following journals for publishing previous versions of these poems:

"I speak not your language, she said to the boy" and
"Omar Abdalmajeed As'ad of Jiljilya"
    The Wrath-Bearing Tree

"Carolina//Al-Tuwani"
    Rise Up Review

"The glass blower"
    The Last Stanza Poetry Journal

"Fourteen trees on Ben Gurion Boulevard or Interment"
    South Carolina Bards Poetry Anthology 2023

I am grateful to all my teachers but primarily to my close mentors Toby Altman and Elizabeth Robinson. Their generosity, guidance, and unwavering support has helped me find my voice and stay the course.

I also have deep gratitude to all my friends, fellow poets, and especially my husband David who patiently and lovingly tuned in to hear my voice.

Also Available from Cathexis Northwest Press:

Something To Cry About
by Robert Krantz

Suburban Hermeneutics
by Ian Cappelli

God's Love Is Very Busy
by David Seung

that one time we were almost people
by Christian Czaniecki

Fever Dream/Take Heart
by Valyntina Grenier

The Book of Night & Waking
by Clif Mason

Dead Birds of New Zealand
by Christian Czaniecki

The Weathering of Igneous Rockforms in High-Altitude Riparian Environments
by John Belk

If A Fish
by George Burns

How to Draw a Blank
by Collin Van Son

En Route
by Jesse Wolfe

sky bright psalms
by Temple Cone

Moonbird
by Henry G. Stanton

southern athiest. oh, honey
by d. e. fulford

Bruises, Birthmarks & Other Calamities
by Nadine Klassen

Wanted: Comedy, Addicts
by AR Dugan

They Curve Like Snakes
by David Alexander McFarland

the catalog of daily fears
by Beth Dufford

Shops Close Too Early
by Josh Feit

Vanity Unfair and Other Poems
by Robert Eugene Rubino

Destructive Heresies
by Milo E. Gorgevska

Bodies of Separation
by Chim Sher Ting

The Night with James Dean and Other Prose Poems
by Allison A. deFreese

About Time
by Julie Benesh

The Unempty Spaces Between
by Louis Efron

Quomodo probatur in conflatorio
by Nick Roberts

Suspended
by Ellen White Rook

Call Me Not Ishmael but the Sea
by J. Martin Daughtry

Wild Evolution
by Naomi Leimsider

Coming To Terms
by Peter Sagnella

Acta
by Patrick Wilcox

Honeymoon Shoes
by Valyntina Grenier

Practising Ascending
by Nadine Hitchiner

LA CUIDAD EN TI: THE CITY WITHIN YOU
by Karla Marrufo
Translated from the Spanish by Allison A. deFreese

Cathexis Northwest Press

www.ingramcontent.com/pod-product-compliance
Lightning Source LLC
Chambersburg PA
CBHW030140100526
44592CB00011B/971